Author Bio

Cher L. Randle is a woman transformed by the healing, restoring, and life-changing power of Jesus Christ. After years of searching for love, identity, and purpose in the wrong places, Cher experienced a radical spiritual awakening at the age of 47 that changed the course of her life forever. Today, she boldly shares her testimony to help women discover their true worth, break generational cycles, and walk confidently in their God-given identity.

Cher is an evangelist, a speaker, and the founder of Evangelist Cher Randle Ministries, where she empowers women through biblical teaching, mentorship, and faith-based encouragement. Her signature message—"Jesus Is the Answer! That's it! That's ALL!"—has resonated with countless women seeking hope, healing, and restoration.

Known for her realness, compassion, and powerful storytelling, Cher ministers from a place of transparency and truth. She believes every woman has a purpose, every pain has a lesson, and every story has the power to set someone else free. Her passion is helping women rise from brokenness into boldness through Christ.

Cher is also a devoted wife, mother, grandmother, and leader in her church community, serving with humility and grace. Her life's mission is simple: to point people to Jesus, to be a living testimony of His love, and to remind every woman that God can awaken beauty from any place of brokenness.

MY REASON WHY

THIS BOOK IS DEDICATED TO MY REASON WHY.

TO MY HUSBAND, THANK YOU FOR LOVING ME THROUGH EVERY SEASON — THE BROKEN DAYS, THE BECOMING DAYS, AND THE AWAKENED DAYS. YOUR SUPPORT, PATIENCE, AND PRAYERS GAVE ME STRENGTH WHEN I DIDN'T HAVE WORDS.

TO MY MOTHER, YOU ARE THE FOUNDATION OF WHO I AM. YOUR SACRIFICES, YOUR FAITH, AND YOUR UNWAVERING LOVE PLANTED SEEDS IN ME LONG BEFORE I UNDERSTOOD MY PURPOSE. I CARRY YOU WITH ME IN EVERYTHING I DO.

TO MY CHILDREN, YOU ARE MY HEART WALKING OUTSIDE MY BODY. EVERY PAGE WRITTEN, EVERY PRAYER PRAYED, AND EVERY STEP TAKEN WAS WITH YOU IN MIND. YOU ARE MY MOTIVATION TO HEAL, TO GROW, AND TO LIVE FULLY AWAKENED IN CHRIST.

YOU ARE MY REASON. YOU ARE MY WHY

Table Of Contents

Chapter 1 - The woman I use to be Pg. 3

Chapter 2- The woman He lifted Pg. 7

Chapter 3 - The woman He restored Pg. 12

Chapter 4- The woman He encouraged Pg. 15

Chapter 5- H.E.R. Awakening Pg .19

Chapter 6- Living anchored in Christ Pg. 22

Chapter 7- Walking in your God-given identity Pg. 25

Chapter 8- When the enemy fights your awakening Pg. 28

Chapter 9- The power of surrender Pg. 31

Chapter 10- Becoming the woman God saw all along Pg. 34

Chapter 11- Living H.E.R. daily Pg. 37

Chapter 12- A letter to the woman awakening right now Pg. 41

Final Chapter- The awakening prayer Pg. 45

THE WOMAN I USED TO BE

CHAPTER
1

This chapter tells the truth of who I was before Jesus awakened me.
It reveals insecurities many people never knew I carried—and that's okay.
This is the beginning of a beautiful, poetic love story between Jesus and me, one that leads into the glory of God.

Let's take a walk through my transformation and my awakening to H.E.R.

Before Christ awakened me, I lived in a cycle that looked successful on the outside but felt painfully empty on the inside. I was always moving—running from job to job, overworking, overperforming, and overachieving—because I believed my worth came from what I did, not who I was. I made sure I looked good. I made sure I smiled. I made sure everyone around me saw the strong woman, the dependable woman, the woman who had it all together.

But inside… I was hurting.

The truth was, I carried shame about who I was and how I looked.
I didn't feel good enough.
I didn't feel smart enough.
I didn't feel beautiful enough.

The world had convinced me that I didn't belong—that my lack of education disqualified me, that my appearance wasn't their kind of beautiful, that someone like me would always be overlooked, unappreciated, and misunderstood. And because I believed what the world said about me, I positioned myself for disappointment repeatedly. I trusted the wrong people. I depended on the wrong voices. I gave my heart to those who were never equipped to hold it.

Every time I tried to rise, something pulled me back.
Every time I thought I was chosen, I was rejected.
Every time I tried to love, I ended up breaking.

I wasn't living—I was performing.
I wasn't whole—I was pretending.
I wasn't confident—I was covering.

The woman I used to be was a woman searching for worth in everything except God.

But while I was running, pretending, surviving, and searching, God—the One who created me and knew me best—was watching over me. He knew my heart. He knew my wounds. He knew the little girl inside me who had never been affirmed. He understood

"Why do You love me when I don't even love myself?"
"Why do You keep calling me when I keep running?"
"Why haven't You given up on me when I gave up on me long ago?"

I didn't ask because I didn't care—not out of selfishness, but out of wounds. I was broken. I was empty. I was operating from a place of rejection and survival. I didn't know that the God who formed me in my mother's womb still saw beauty in the very places where I saw shame. I didn't know He had placed purpose inside me long before the world tried to tell me who I wasn't. I didn't know the same God who painted the sky had written a destiny over my life that no person, no heartbreak, and no season could cancel.

There comes a moment when the weight becomes too heavy, when the pretending becomes exhausting, when the pain you've been pushing down finally rises to the surface. For me, that moment came slowly—like a quiet storm building inside my soul.

I was tired.
Tired of being strong.
Tired of surviving.
Tired of performing.
Tired of being everything for everyone while no one noticed the cracks forming inside me.

Overachieving no longer filled the emptiness.
The relationships didn't stop the loneliness.
The busyness didn't silence the shame.
The overworking didn't heal the brokenness.

My heart was bruised.
My spirit was drained.
My confidence was gone.

And the truth was...
I didn't even know who I was anymore.

I had given so much of myself away that I no longer recognized the woman staring back at me in the mirror. The sparkle in my eyes was fading. The hope in my heart was slipping. The joy I pretended to have was nothing more than a mask. And beneath that mask was a woman crying:

"Lord, is this really all there is for me?"
"Is this the life I'm supposed to live?"
"Why does love keep breaking me?"
"Why can't I be enough for anyone?"
"Why do I feel invisible, even when I'm giving my all?"

It wasn't a loud cry. It was the kind of cry only God can hear—a soul cry, a tired cry, a "Lord, I can't keep doing this" cry.
And that's when God stepped in.

Not with lightning.
Not with shaking.
Not with fear.

But with mercy.
With love.
With a whisper that felt like a lifeline:

"Daughter, come to Me."

In that moment—when I had nothing else left to give—Jesus came for me. He reached the deepest place of my brokenness, and for the first time in my life, I felt seen. Truly seen. Not for what I did. Not for how I looked. Not for how strong I pretended to be. But for who I truly was:

A daughter.
A woman God loved.
A woman God created.
A woman God had been waiting on.

My breaking point became the doorway to my awakening.

It wasn't that God didn't see me—
I just didn't see myself through Him.

I survived seasons that should have broken me, not knowing they were preparing me for the woman God was awakening.

-Evangelist Cher Randle

THE WOMAN HE LIFTED

CHAPTER

2

Before Christ awakened me, I felt like life had pushed me so far down that I didn't know how to rise again. I wasn't standing in strength—I was standing in survival. Every disappointment pushed me lower. Every betrayal pressed me deeper. Every rejection felt like another weight added to my soul. I was functioning but not living. I was moving but not thriving. I was standing, but only because I didn't have the choice to fall.

But even at my lowest point… God still saw me.

When others overlooked me, He looked at me.
When people used me, He cared for me.
When I felt invisible, He recognized me.
When I felt unworthy, He called me worthy.

I didn't realize it then, but I was not just a woman crying out. I was a woman God was preparing to lift.

He lifted me when I didn't have the strength to lift myself.
He lifted me when I didn't think I deserved it.
He lifted me when I was drowning in my own tears.
He lifted me when I was lost in shame and confusion.

My cry reached heaven, but His hand reached me.

There is a kind of lifting only Jesus can do.
The kind that heals what people never touched and restores what life tried to destroy.

People can encourage you, but they can't heal you.
People can admire you, but they can't restore you.
People can cheer for you, but they can't transform you.

But Jesus!

When He lifts you, everything changes.

He lifted my mind out of lies I had believed for years.
He lifted my heart out of hurt I had carried for too long.
He lifted my spirit out of the pit of rejection and insecurity.
He lifted my identity out of the hands of people who mishandled it.

The world convinced me I wasn't enough, but when Jesus lifted me, I realized the truth:
I am exactly who God says I am.
I am not the woman broken by life—I am the woman strengthened by His love.

I am not the woman left behind—I am the woman chosen by God.
I am not the woman defined by her issues—I am the woman rescued, redeemed, and restored.

When Jesus lifts you, He doesn't just pull you up—He pulls you into truth.
Into identity.

Into purpose.
Into destiny.
Into a love that finally makes sense.

After decades of trying to make life work on my own, God lifted me higher than I had ever stood in my life—not because I was perfect, not because I was strong, and not because I did everything right, but because He loves me.

He lifted me not just out of where I was...
but into who I was always meant to be.

I was no longer the woman people broke—I was the woman He rebuilt.
I was no longer the woman the world rejected—I was the woman He embraced.
I was no longer the woman hiding in pain—I was the woman He awakened.

This is the beauty of Christ:

He doesn't just save you—He lifts you.
He doesn't just forgive you—He restores you.
He doesn't just call you, His daughter.

He teaches you how to walk like one.

That lifting, the moment God raised me from the inside out became the beginning of everything new.

When I began reading the Word and praying for real, something supernatural started happening inside me. Layers of fear began falling off. Lies I had carried for years began breaking. The heaviness in my chest began lifting.

And then, something shifted in my spirit.

I began walking in the authority God gave me, not the identity the world tried to force on me. For the first time in my life, I realized:

I don't belong to the world. I belong to God. And if I belong to God, then I have access to everything He promised me.

I started seeing myself differently, not through the lens of my past, my pain, or my performance, but through the truth of who God says I am. What once defined me no longer held the same power. As my relationship with Christ deepened, my strength was no longer rooted in myself, but in Him. I wasn't trying to prove anything anymore. I was learning how to walk in what God had already spoken over my life.

That scripture woke something up inside me.

For years, the world had spoken limits over my life—reminding me of everything I supposedly couldn't do:

You're not educated enough.
You're not pretty enough.

You're not chosen.
You're not qualified.
Stay in your place.
Don't aim too high.

But the moment God lifted me, He spoke something different:

"Daughter, you can do ALL things—because I strengthen you."

My worth was no longer rooted in their opinions.
My worth became rooted in Christ, who is my strength.

And when Christ is your strength, you walk differently.
You talk differently.
You think differently.
You believe differently.
You fight differently.
You rise differently.

That's when I realized—God didn't just lift me; He empowered me.

Here is the truth every woman needs to understand:
Faith and hope in Jesus' lead to trust in Jesus. You cannot trust a God you do not know. You cannot walk in authority without relationship. You cannot stand in power without prayer. You cannot fight spiritually without the Word.

It takes a relationship to know His heart.
It takes a relationship to hear His voice.
It takes a relationship to trust His timing.
It takes a relationship to understand your identity in Him.

And a relationship is built by fasting, praying, and studying God's Word.

Fasting is where you quiet your flesh so you can hear God more clearly. It is not about punishment or performance, it is about positioning your heart to listen, surrender, and realign with His will.

Prayer is not a speech, it is intimacy, communication, access, and honesty. It is where God comforts your spirit, reveals His plans, and builds your trust.

The Word is how you learn who He is. The Bible is not just a book—it is God introducing Himself to you. "In the beginning was the Word, and the Word was with God, and the Word WAS God."

Every time I opened the Bible, God opened Himself to me.

And the more I got to know Him, the more I wanted Him.

The more I trusted Him.
The more I surrendered.
The more I healed.
The more I changed.

Little by little.
Step by step.
Tear by tear.
Scripture by scripture...

The broken woman began walking in authority.
The rejected woman began walking in confidence.
The wounded woman began walking in purpose.
The insecure woman began walking in identity.

And the woman He lifted became the woman Jesus awakened—because Jesus had been the Answer all along.

When I could no longer lift myself, God reached down and reminded me that His strength is made perfect in my weakness.

-Evangelist Cher Randle

THE WOMAN HE RESTORED

CHAPTER

3

Restoration is not sudden. It doesn't happen in a moment, and it doesn't happen all at once. God does not rush what He loves, and He does not patch broken pieces—He rebuilds them. Looking back now, I realize He didn't just lift me out of my pain; He began restoring me from the inside out. And He started with the part of me that had been damaged the longest: my mind.

For years, my thoughts were shaped by rejection, disappointment, insecurity, and other people's opinions. I believed lies about myself—lies planted by the world, watered by experiences, and reinforced by heartbreak. But when God stepped into my life at forty-seven, He didn't just change my circumstances—He started changing my thinking. Restoration began the moment He started replacing every lie with His truth. Slowly, gently, and consistently, He whispered to my heart, You are enough. You are chosen. You are loved. You are Mine.

I didn't know it then, but each time I opened my Bible, Jesus was meeting me there renewing my mind and teaching me to see myself the way He saw me.

As my mind began to heal, God moved to the next place I didn't even realize needed attention: my heart. My heart had been shattered so many times that I became numb to the cracks. I didn't recognize that I was operating with a heart covered in bruises. But God saw every wound. He knew every moment that had shaped me. And instead of rushing me to "get over it," He patiently restored the tender places I had learned to ignore.

He loved me with a love I didn't understand at first—steady, gentle, unwavering, and holy. It was the kind of love that didn't hurt me, didn't confuse me, didn't abandon me, and didn't change based on my performance. His love healed memories I avoided, softened the hardness I carried, and settled peace over the places where chaos once lived.

As He restored my heart, He restored something even deeper—my identity. I had spent most of my life defining myself by what others said, by the mistakes I made, and by the failures I lived through. I believed I wasn't enough because that's what life had taught me. But God began showing me that I was not the names life gave me; I was the name He gave me.

Little by little, He reminded me that I was His daughter, His creation, His vessel, His warrior, His chosen woman. When God restores you, He does not restore you back to who you used to be—He restores you into who He originally created you to be. He brings you back to your true identity, the one that existed before pain ever touched you.

And with identity came faith—real faith. Not the faith I said I had or tried to force, but a faith built through every moment God proved Himself. My faith didn't grow because life became easier; it grew because God became clearer. Every prayer I whispered, He answered in ways I didn't expect. Every tear I cried, He caught long before it fell. Every moment I doubted, He reassured me with peace. My faith grew because I finally saw God for who He truly is: a Father who does not fail
.
As He restored my faith, He restored my purpose. The woman I used to be had dreams that died young. The woman He lifted had hope again. But the woman He restored began walking in a calling I never imagined for myself. I began to understand that everything I had endured was preparing me for everything God was calling me to.

He restored my voice so I could speak to others. He restored my confidence so I could stand boldly in the places He assigned to me. He restored my strength so I could carry the mantle He placed on my life. And He restored my heart so I could love people the way He loves me.

I realized something powerful: I was not restored for myself—I was restored for His glory. The woman He restored is not the same woman life tried to break. I am stronger, wiser, softer, and louder. I am healed, awakened, and covered in purpose.

Restoration is not just God putting you back together—it is God revealing who you were always meant to be. And the woman He restored is the woman I am finally becoming

 And I know now that this restoration did not come from time, effort, or strength of my own. It came through Jesus Christ, the One who met me in my brokenness and walked me through every stage of healing. God restored me through Jesus—the Answer who renewed my mind, healed my heart, and awakened my purpose.

Restoration did not erase my scars; it redeemed them and gave them purpose.

-Evangelist Cher Randle

THE WOMAN HE ENCOURAGED

CHAPTER

4

Restoration opened my eyes, but encouragement strengthened my steps. Once God began healing my mind, my heart, and my identity, I realized something profound— He didn't just want me to be restored; He wanted me to be encouraged. He wanted me to walk with confidence, with boldness, and with an assurance that I was no longer the woman I used to be.

Encouragement from God hits different...

It doesn't flatter your ego—
it strengthens your spirit.
It doesn't puff you up—
it builds you up.
It doesn't fade with emotion—
it anchors you in truth.

God began speaking to me in ways I couldn't ignore. Some days it was through scripture. Other days it was through quiet whispers in my heart. And sometimes it was through a simple moment—sunlight warming my face, a song at the right time, a thought that came out of nowhere yet settled my entire soul. That was God reminding me, "Daughter, you're not alone. I'm with you."

The more I leaned into Him, the more He revealed Himself. The more I prayed, the more I heard Him. The more I read His Word, the more I understood His voice. And in every step of that process, God was encouraging me—strengthening me to become the woman He always knew I could be.

There were days when I questioned my purpose. Days when I wondered if I was truly qualified. Days when my past tried to pull me back into old insecurities. But God had a way of lifting my chin and speaking directly to the parts of me that wanted to shrink.

I remember one day in prayer, I asked Him, "Lord, why me? Why would You call a woman like me?"
And in the quiet of that moment, He answered my heart:
"Because I can trust you with what I've brought you through."

That's encouragement.
That's love.
That's God.

He reminded me that brokenness doesn't disqualify you— it qualifies you. It prepares you to see others the way God sees them. It prepares you to speak life because you know what it feels like to be dying inside. It prepares you to lift others because you know the weight of falling.

Encouragement became my fuel. It was God's way of saying, "Keep going. You're on the right path. I restored you for a reason."

There were moments when old thoughts tried to creep back in—the thoughts that said I wasn't enough, that I didn't belong, that my past was too messy. But every time those lies rose up, God met me with His truth. His Word became my reassurance, my foundation, my steady place.

I began to feel something I had never truly felt before—courage.
Not the kind of courage that comes from pride or performance, but the kind that comes from knowing God is with you. The kind that rises up when the enemy tries to whisper doubt. The kind that makes you stand tall even when your knees want to buckle.
I started believing that I could do what God was calling me to do.

I started believing that I was enough.
I started believing that I was chosen.
I started believing that I was appointed for this season.
And that belief didn't come from me—
it came from Him.

God encouraged me through His Word, speaking life into the places where death once lived. He encouraged me through prayer, strengthening the parts of me that had been weak for too long. He encouraged me through His presence, reminding me that even when I felt alone, I was never abandoned.

Encouragement is not just God patting you on the back.
It is God preparing you for purpose.

It is God saying.
"Stand up, daughter. I restored you so you can move forward."

I learned that encouragement helps you walk differently. It's what helps you speak boldly. It's what helps you show up for your assignment with confidence. Encouragement from God becomes the wind behind your wings—the push that propels you into destiny.

And the more He encouraged me, the more I realized that He wasn't just restoring my life—He was restoring my voice. The voice that had been silent by rejection. The voice that had been muted by insecurity. The voice that had been buried beneath years of survival.

He encouraged me so I could encourage others.

He strengthened me so I could strengthen others.

He breathed life into me so I could breathe life into women who felt just like I once did—broken, tired, unseen, and unloved.

The woman He encouraged became the woman ready to walk in purpose.

The woman He encouraged became the woman ready to walk in purpose.

I now understand that this encouragement did not come from emotion or self-confidence—it came through Jesus Christ. Jesus was the One strengthening my steps, steadying my faith, and reminding me that I was never walking alone. Jesus was—and still is—the Answer.

God's encouragement met me in my lowest moments and whispered, "You are not finished yet."

-Evangelist Cher Randle

H.E.R. AWAKENING

CHAPTER 5

Now that Christ has awakened me, I am renewed—truly renewed. The woman I am today does not look like the woman I used to be. My thoughts have shifted. My heart has shifted. My vision has shifted. Life looks different through these awakened eyes. What once felt confusing now feels purposeful. What once felt heavy now feels holy.

Just as the Word says, "Eye has not seen, nor ear heard, nor have entered into the heart of man the things which God has prepared for those who love Him." And now I know—deep in my spirit—that God has prepared more for me than I ever imagined. More joy. More peace. More purpose. More wisdom. More encounters. More transformation.

My awakening taught me something I wish I had learned sooner:
There is more to life than the lies we see on social media.
There is more than comparison, validation chasing, appearance-keeping, pretending, and competing.

Life is not about proving yourself—it is about living like Christ.
To truly live is to reflect Him.
To love without conditions.
To walk with compassion.
To show kindness even when it is not returned.
To help someone who cannot repay you.
To be a comforter, not a critic.
To build others up, not tear them down.
To shine light where darkness once lived.
To live the life God created for you—intentionally, joyfully, and thankfully.

My awakening did not make life perfect.
It made life purposeful.

Now, I embrace the trials—
because trials mean Jesus is with me.
Trials mean growth.
Trials mean elevation.
Trials mean God is working in places I cannot yet see.

I no longer run from the process.
I walk through it with Him.

This awakening also taught me something many women need to hear:

It is time to move in the purpose God has given you.
Not the purpose the world tells you to chase.
Not the purpose social media celebrates.
Not the purpose rooted in "girl power," independence, or self-made hype.

We do not need more girl power.
We need more JESUS power.

Girl power fades.
But the power of Jesus sustains.
Transforms.
Heals.
Delivers.
Restores.
And awakens.

Everything I am today is because of Him.
I would not have made it this far without Him.
I could not have survived the storms without Him.
I cannot imagine moving forward in this life without knowing Him.

My awakening is simple, yet supernatural:
I am healed by His stripes.
I am edified by His love.
I am restored by His grace.
I am covered by His blood.
I am strengthened by His presence.
I am guided by His Spirit.

I am she—
the woman Christ awakened,
the woman He renewed,
the woman He set free,
the woman living H.E.R. Awakening by His power.

This is my testimony.
This is my transformation.
This is my awakening.

And I pray that as you read my story,
you begin to feel yours rising too.

My awakening began the moment I stopped searching for answers and surrendered to Jesus.

-Evangelist Cher Randle

Living Anchored in Christ

CHAPTER

6

People often ask me, "How do you do it? How do you stay strong? How do you keep showing up with joy, peace, and purpose? And every time I hear that question, I smile.

Not because I have a perfect life, and not because everything is easy, but because the answer is so simple it confuses those expecting something deep, long, or impressive.

The answer is Jesus.
Just Jesus.
Jesus is the Answer.
That's it. That's all.

I don't stand because I have strength of my own. I stand because I am anchored—anchored in Christ, anchored in His Word, anchored in His promises, anchored in His love. Before my awakening, I was tossed by every emotion, every disappointment, every betrayal, and every fear. One wrong look, one wrong word, one rejection could send me spiraling. I was unsteady, unstable, and uncertain because my life wasn't rooted in anything that could truly hold me.

But when Christ awakened me, everything shifted. He became my anchor—not an accessory, not an emergency contact, not a Sunday habit, but my foundation. And when Christ becomes your foundation, the structure of your life changes. Storms still come, but they no longer destroy you. Trials still happen, but they no longer shake you loose. You still cry, but you don't crumble. You still hurt, but you don't lose hope. You still walk through fire, but you come out without the smell of smoke.

That's what it means to be anchored.

People see strength, the glow, the peace, and the confidence, but they don't always see the root. They see the fruit, but not the foundation. They see the woman standing tall, but not the Savior holding her steady. And that's why, when people ask how I do what I do, I give them the only honest answer I have: by the grace of God.

Jesus is how I breathe.
Jesus is how I survive.
Jesus is how I stay sane.
Jesus is how I stay whole.

He is the strength behind my smile, the peace within my storms, the light in my darkest valleys, and the reason I made it through seasons that should have destroyed me. I couldn't have come this far without Him, and I can't imagine living one day forward without knowing Him.

Living anchored in Christ changed how I see the world. I no longer view life through pressure, competition, comparison, or insecurity. Life is more than what we see on social media. Life is deeper than the highlights people post. True living is Christ-like living—loving without conditions, walking in compassion, showing kindness, helping someone who can't repay you, being a comforter instead of a critic, and carrying His presence into every space you enter.

Anchored living taught me to appreciate the life God created for me and to embrace the trials He allows—because trials mean Jesus is with me. Trials grow me. Trials stretch me. Trials prepare me. Trials reveal what is planted in me. And trials prove that no matter what comes against me, Christ holds me firmly in place.

Being anchored made me bold enough to walk in my purpose—not the purpose the world pushes, but the purpose God assigned to my name. This awakening taught me to release the "girl power" mindset the world celebrates. Because girl power can only push you so far—but Jesus power transforms. Jesus power sustains. Jesus power heals. Jesus power delivers.

Jesus power awakens.

Everything I am today is because of Him.
Everything I've survived is because of Him.
Everything I will become is anchored in Him.

My awakening revealed my truth:
I am healed by His stripes.
I am edified by His love.
I am restored by His grace.

I am she—
the woman Christ awakened,
the woman Christ renewed,
the woman Christ restored.

Living out H.E.R. Awakening—
not by my strength,
but by His.

When Christ became my anchor, the storms no longer defined me.

-Evangelist Cher Randle

WALKING IN YOUR GOD-GIVEN IDENTITY

CHAPTER

7

When Christ awakened me, I not only stepped out of the darkness I had lived in for so many years—I stepped into a new identity. It felt unfamiliar at first, like slipping into a pair of shoes I wasn't used to wearing. But the more I learned about who God said I was, the more I realized how much I had been living beneath my calling, beneath my purpose, and beneath my worth.

For most of my life, I allowed others to define me. I let rejection write its labels on me. I let insecurities shape how I saw myself. I let my past determine how I showed up in rooms. I let brokenness convince me that I was unqualified for anything better. And for a long time, I believed the lie that I was whatever life had made me.

But awakening changes your vision.
Awakening reveals truth.
Awakening exposes every false identity you ever accepted.

As I walked deeper with Christ, I began to discover a version of myself I never knew existed—the version He created long before pain ever touched me.

The more I read His Word, the more I prayed, the more I listened for His voice, the clearer it became:

There is confidence that comes with that truth—not a loud confidence, but a steady one.
A confidence that doesn't need to prove anything to anyone.
A confidence that doesn't beg to be seen, chosen, or validated.
A confidence rooted not in performance, but in belonging.

Walking in my God-given identity meant I no longer needed to chase the approval I once craved. It meant releasing the pressure to be perfect. It meant I didn't have to hide behind a mask of strength anymore. I was allowed to grow, allowed to heal, allowed to change, and allowed to walk away from anything that tried to pull me back into who I used to be.

There were moments when old insecurities tried to whisper—reminding me of mistakes, moments of weakness, or wounds not fully closed. But identity is stronger than insecurity. The voice of God is louder than the voice of fear. The truth of who I am in Christ silences every lie of who I was in the world.

Every time I doubted myself, God reminded me:
"You are Mine."

Every time fear tried to creep in, He whispered:
"I am with you."

Every time the enemy tried to pull me backward, God stood firm and declared:
"You are chosen."

Identity is not a feeling—it is a foundation.
It is where purpose begins.
It is the truth that builds you, strengthens you, and makes you unshakable.

For the first time in my life, I was walking as the woman God always knew I could be—not the woman life shaped out of pain, but the woman He shaped out of love. And with every step I took in alignment with Him, my identity grew stronger, clearer, and more rooted in His truth.

Jesus made that identity possible.
Through Christ, I learned who I am—and who I am not.
Through Him, my worth was restored, my confidence was grounded, and my identity was secured.

I no longer ask the world who I am.
I no longer allow broken people to define me.
I no longer shrink myself to fit into places God never assigned me.

I walk in my identity boldly now—
because I finally know who I am,
and more importantly,
I know Whose I am—
in Christ.

I stopped trying to become who the world expected and embraced who God had already called me to be.

-Evangelist Cher Randle

WHEN THE ENEMY FIGHTS YOUR AWAKENING

CHAPTER
8

Awakening doesn't go unnoticed. The moment Christ lifted me, restored me, and began revealing who I truly was, the enemy became threatened—not because of who I had been, but because of who I was becoming. A healed woman is dangerous. A woman with identity is dangerous. A woman who knows her worth in Christ is dangerous. And a woman walking in her purpose? She is a direct threat to hell.

After God awakened me, I expected peace. I expected joy. I expected clarity. What I didn't expect was the warfare. I didn't expect the enemy to fight so hard. I didn't expect old thoughts to try to return, old feelings to rise up, or the spiritual pressure that comes when God elevates your spirit.

But the enemy fights what he fears.

The moment God lifted me out, the enemy tried to pull me back in.
The moment God restored me, the enemy tried to remind me of who I used to be.
The moment God poured identity into me, the enemy whispered lies about my past.
The moment God gave me purpose, the enemy threw distractions at my feet.

He fought me in my mind first.

Old insecurities tried to speak again.
Old wounds tried to reopen.
Old heartbreaks tried to replay themselves.
Old fears tried to convince me I wasn't really changed.

But awakening taught me this:

If the enemy is fighting you, God is forming you.
Warfare is not a sign that God has left you.
Warfare is a sign that the enemy sees your growth.
Warfare is confirmation that you are moving into destiny.

Before Christ, I would have fallen apart under pressure. I would have run back to old patterns, old people, and old coping mechanisms. But this time was different. This time, I had something I had never had before—an anchor. And that anchor held me together when everything around me tried to pull me apart.

The enemy tried to attack my identity, but I knew who I was now.
The enemy tried to attack my peace, but Christ had spoken calm into places where storms once lived.
The enemy tried to attack my confidence, but I had learned to see myself through God's eyes.

The enemy wanted me to forget my awakening, but God kept reminding me of His hand on my life. Even when the attacks felt intense, something in me stayed steady —not because I was strong, but because I was no longer fighting alone. Jesus was standing with me, speaking to my spirit, steadying my steps, calming my heart, and reminding me of everything He had promised.

Warfare didn't break me—it built me.
It made me pray harder.
It made me stand stronger.
It made me trust deeper.
It made me love God more fiercely.
It made my purpose clearer.

A woman who has survived spiritual warfare with Christ beside her becomes unshakable. She becomes confident. She becomes bold. She becomes wise. She becomes spiritually alert. She becomes the kind of woman who walks into a room and hell takes notice.

The enemy didn't fight me because I was weak.
He fought me because I was awakening.
He fought me because I was healing.
He fought me because I was rising.
He fought me because I was stepping into everything God destined for me.

But every attack, every lie, every moment of pressure proved one thing:

Jesus was covering me.
Jesus was strengthening me.
Jesus was fighting for me.

Warfare didn't stop my awakening.

It strengthened it—because Christ carried me through it.

Resistance did not mean I was losing; it meant my awakening was a threat.

-Evangelist Cher Randle

THE POWER OF SURRENDER

CHAPTER

9

There comes a point in every awakening when you realize that healing and restoration are only the beginning. God doesn't awaken you just to show you who you are—He awakens you so you can surrender who you were. And surrender, I learned, is not a moment. It's a posture. A lifestyle. A decision you wake up and choose over and over again.

Before Christ awakened me, surrender was a word I didn't fully understand. I thought surrender meant weakness, loss of control, giving up, or being powerless. But as God began peeling back the layers of my heart, I realized surrender was actually the most powerful thing I could ever offer Him.

Surrender means trusting God more than your own understanding.
It means letting go of what hurt you so God can heal what's left.
It means releasing the people you wanted to hold on to so God can bring the ones meant for your destiny.
It means laying down your will so His will can rise in you.

What I didn't know then was that surrender is what separates survival from transformation. You can't go deeper in God while holding onto pieces of your old life. You can't walk in your purpose with your hands full of the past. You can't rise while still gripping what keeps you low.

Surrender requires honesty.
Honesty about what hurt you.
Honesty about what lied to you.
Honesty about what you're afraid to release.
Honesty about who you used to be and who God is calling you to become.

When I began to surrender for real, it felt like God was asking for everything I thought I needed to survive—my pride, my defenses, my independence, my need for control, my fear of being hurt again. It was scary at first. I had lived so long protecting myself that letting God in felt like stepping into the unknown. But every time I laid something down, He replaced it with something better.

When I surrendered old pain, He gave me peace.
When I surrendered insecurity, He gave me confidence in Him.
When I surrendered loneliness, He filled me with His presence.
When I surrendered control, He opened doors I could never have unlocked on my own.

I learned that you cannot lose when you surrender to God.
You only gain.

You gain clarity.
You gain direction.
You gain healing.
You gain identity.
You gain wisdom and strength.
You gain everything that truly matters.

Surrender is also where obedience lives. When God tells you to move, you move. When He tells you to let go, you let go. When He tells you to forgive, you forgive. When He tells you to trust Him, you do it—even when it doesn't make sense. Because surrender teaches you that God is always working behind the scenes, preparing something greater than what you are releasing.

And here is the truth I wish more people understood:

You are never fully awakened until you are surrendered.
Awakening opens your eyes, but surrender opens your life.
Awakening shows you God, but surrender lets God show you yourself.
Awakening changes your vision, but surrender changes your direction.

The moment I surrendered completely, I felt a freedom I had never known. Everything that once weighed me down became light. My breathing felt easier. My thoughts became clearer. My spirit grew steadier. I wasn't wrestling with God anymore—I was walking with Him.

I discovered that surrender is not losing control; it is giving control to the One who knows exactly what to do with my life. It is choosing peace over panic. Faith over fear. Trust over doubt. God's truth over my feelings. And His purpose over my plans.

Surrender is where Jesus met me most deeply.

When I laid everything at His feet, He carried what I could not.
Through Christ, I learned that surrender is not weakness—it is strength anchored in Him.

Surrender is where I found the strongest version of myself.
Not the version built by survival—
but the version shaped by God's hands, God's timing, God's love, and God's grace.

The woman I am today stands strong not because she has everything figured out, but because she has surrendered everything to Jesus, the One who does. And surrender, I now know, is not a sacrifice—it is an invitation into everything God has prepared for me.

Surrender was not giving up — it was trusting God enough to let Him take over.

-Evangelist Cher Randle

BECOMING THE WOMAN GOD SAW ALL ALONG

CHAPTER

10

Becoming is a journey. It is not rushed, not forced, not manufactured—it is revealed. Becoming is what happens when surrender meets purpose. It unfolds when God removes the layers life has placed on you and begins revealing the version of yourself, He always had in mind.

For many years, I lived as the woman circumstances shaped.
The woman heartbreak built.
The woman insecurities molded.
The woman rejection sculpted.
The woman pain convinced I had to be.

I didn't know there was another version of me hidden beneath survival. I didn't know God had been holding a blueprint of my life long before I ever took my first breath.

But once Christ awakened me and I surrendered, He began walking me toward the woman He saw all along.

Becoming didn't happen overnight. It didn't come in a single moment. It didn't arrive through one prayer, one scripture, or one encounter. Becoming happened gradually, quietly, and intentionally like a sunrise unveiling light little by little, pushing back darkness one shade at a time.

I noticed shifts in me.
Small ones at first.
Then bigger ones.
Then undeniable ones.

I spoke differently.
I listened differently.
I prayed differently.
I forgave differently.
I loved differently.
I showed up differently.
I carried myself differently.
I saw myself differently.

And as I changed, I realized something profound:

I wasn't just growing. I was returning.

Returning to the woman God originally created.
Returning to the woman who lived beneath the pain.
Returning to the woman who survived every storm.
Returning to the woman who had purpose before she had problems.
Returning to the woman God whispered over before the world ever wounded her.

Becoming the woman God saw all along required letting go of the false versions of myself I accepted out of fear and brokenness. It required releasing lies I lived under for years. It required forgiving myself for the woman I used to be. It required grace for the woman I was becoming.

Some days I didn't feel strong.
Some days I didn't feel awakened.
Some days I didn't feel transformed.

But becoming is not about feeling—it is about forming.

God was forming something in me the old version of myself could not hold. He was forming resilience. He was forming wisdom. He was forming spiritual maturity. He was forming compassion. He was forming confidence. He was forming strength rooted not in independence, but in Him.

One of the most beautiful parts of becoming was realizing that God had always seen this version of me—even when I couldn't see it myself. He saw the healed me when I was still broken. He saw the confident me when insecurity was all I knew. He saw the bold me when I was afraid of my own voice. He saw the loving me when all I understood was hurt. He saw the restored me when shame told me I wasn't worthy of restoration.

God saw me whole before I ever understood wholeness.
He saw me standing before I knew how to rise.
He saw me shining before I stepped out of the shadows.
He saw me victorious before I ever faced the battle.
He saw me awakened before I ever knew I was asleep.

Becoming the woman God saw all along also meant embracing responsibility. Healing gave me freedom, but becoming gave me assignment. God didn't transform me for myself alone—He transformed me because someone needed the version of me who walked through fire and came out with a testimony. Someone needed my voice. Someone needed my story. Someone needed to see what Jesus Christ can do with a surrendered life.

This chapter of my life is not just about who I am—
it is about who God is through Christ in me.

And that is why becoming will always be one of the most sacred parts of my awakening. Because I am still becoming. Still evolving. Still growing. Still learning. Still being shaped by the hands that molded me from the beginning.
I am no longer the woman life tried to make me.
I am the woman God always saw.
I am the woman God always called.
I am the woman God always loved.
I am the woman Jesus awakened, restored, and redeemed.
Jesus is the Answer—then, now, and always.

God did not change my identity; He revealed it.

-Evangelist Cher Randle

LIVING H.E.R. DAILY

CHAPTER

11

Healing, Encouragement, and Restoration are not just moments in my story—they are the lifestyle God has called me to live every single day.

H.E.R. Awakening is not a one-time encounter or a single breakthrough. It is a daily decision, a daily posture, and a daily walk with God.

There was a time when I believed healing only happened in big moments such as a powerful prayer, a church service, a tear-filled night at the altar. I thought restoration had to be dramatic, instant, or emotional.

And encouragement? I believed it had to come from others, as if it was something I had to wait for.

But living awakened taught me differently.

Healing happens in the small moments too.
In the way you speak to yourself.
In the grace you give your own heart.
In the boundaries you finally establish.
In the thoughts you reject because you know better now.

Healing is in the pause before you react.

It's in the way you protect your peace.
It's in the forgiveness you extend—not because they deserve it, but because you deserve freedom.

Encouragement is something I learned to speak over my own life. I could no longer wait for others to lift me. I had to learn to lift myself in the Lord, even when I didn't feel strong. Even when no one understood my journey. Even when I was standing alone.

Encouragement became a language—a spiritual posture where I reminded myself of who I am, who I am becoming, and who God promised I would be. Some days, encouragement sounded like a whisper. Other days, it sounded like a declaration. But every day, it was necessary.

And restoration...

Restoration is continually unfolding.
It's not a moment it's a movement.

God doesn't restore just once. He keeps restoring as you grow.
He keeps renewing as you walk.
He keeps reshaping you as you surrender deeper into His will.

Living H.E.R. daily means waking up as a healed woman—even on days when old thoughts try to pull you back into brokenness. It means choosing encouragement over doubt, even when you feel tired. It means standing in restoration, even when life tries to remind you of who you used to be.

There are days when the past tries to whisper.
There are days when the enemy tries to provoke old wounds.
There are days when people try to pull you into old patterns.

But H.E.R. isn't just what happened to me who I am now.

I am a healed woman learning to protect the healing God gave me.
I am an encouraged woman learning to speak life into every season.
I am a restored woman learning to rise boldly into my purpose.

Living H.E.R. means your decisions align with your destiny instead of your history. It means you walk with confidence, not arrogance. You love with wisdom, not fear. You serve with compassion, not exhaustion. You show up in rooms as your true self—not the version the world tried to create, but the version God awakened.

Some mornings, healing is loud, you feel it, see it, and walk in it with strength. Other mornings, healing is quiet—it looks like choosing peace, choosing joy, choosing forgiveness, or choosing patience. But whether loud or quiet, it is still healing. It is still God at work in you.

Encouragement begins when you remember who holds your story.
Restoration deepens when you accept that you are not who you used to be.

Living H.E.R. daily is the evidence that Jesus didn't just lift you—

He keeps lifting you.
He keeps guiding you.
He keeps growing you.
He keeps loving you.
He keeps awakening you.

And as you live it day by day, something beautiful happens:
You become the example.
You become the breakthrough someone else needs.
You become the testimony someone else stands on.
You become the encouragement someone else has been praying for.

Living H.E.R. daily is not about perfection—it is about the presence of Jesus Christ.

It is about walking with Jesus Christ in everything you do, everything you choose, and everything you become.

I don't live by chance anymore.
I live by Christ.

I don't live by fear anymore.
I live by faith.

I don't live from my old wounds.
I live from my renewed identity.

H.E.R. is not just my story—
it is my lifestyle now.

And every day, I choose to live awakened.

Healing, encouragement, and restoration are not destinations; they are daily decisions.

-Evangelist Cher Randle

A LETTER TO THE WOMAN
AWAKENING RIGHT NOW

CHAPTER

12

To the woman holding this book in her hands,

I don't know your name.
I don't know your story.
I don't know what you've survived, what you've carried, or what you've been silently battling.

But I know this:

You are not reading these words by accident.

You are here because God is awakening something in you—something powerful, something deep, something holy, something you may not even have language for yet.

I want you to know that I see you.
And even more importantly—God sees you.
He sees the strength you don't give yourself credit for.
He sees the tears you never talked about.
He sees the pieces of you you've been trying to hold together on your own.
He sees the smile you wear while your heart quietly aches.
He sees the way you show up for others, even when no one shows up for you.
He sees the battle behind your eyes that you've learned to hide so well.

And I need you to hear this:

There is nothing wrong with you.
You're not broken—you're awakening.

You are awakening from the lies that tried to shape you.
Awakening from the hurt that tried to silence you.
Awakening from the insecurity that tried to cage you.
Awakening from the rejection that tried to define you.
Awakening from the pain that tried to convince you you were unworthy.
Awakening from the fear that tried to steal your future.

You are not failing—you are transforming.
You are not lost—you are being found by the One who created you.

I know what it feels like to be tired.
Tired of pretending.
Tired of being strong for everyone else.
Tired of carrying wounds that never healed right.
Tired of hoping things will get better and feeling disappointed again.
Tired of searching for love in the wrong places.
Tired of fighting battles that wear you down spiritually and emotionally.

But even in your exhaustion, God is calling you gently.

He's not shouting.
He's not condemning.
He's not pushing.

He's whispering:

"Daughter, come to Me."

You do not have to fix yourself before you come to Him.
You do not have to understand everything at once.
You do not have to be perfect, polished, or healed.

Awakening begins right where you are—
with whatever you have,
with whatever strength is left,
with whatever hope you can still hold.

Let me tell you something I learned the hard way:

Awakening is not about what you feel—it's about what God is doing.

Some days you will feel strong.
Other days you will feel fragile.
Some days you will feel free.
Other days you will feel like you're fighting old battles.

But no matter how you feel—God is working.
In the background.
In the silence.
In the nights when you cry.
In the mornings when you feel numb.
In the moments when you want to give up.

He is awakening something in you that hell cannot stop.

So, to the woman reading this—
You will rise again.
You will feel joy again.
You will love again.
You will hope again.
You will breathe again.

You will see yourself the way God sees you—
beautiful, powerful, chosen, and full of purpose.

You are not behind.
You are not forgotten.
You are not alone.
You are not disqualified.

You are not too broken.
You are not too late.

You are awakening.

And the same God who awakened me
is awakening you—through Jesus Christ.

So take a deep breath.
Loosen your shoulders.
Let the tears fall if they need to.
Lift your chin.
Open your heart.

You don't have to understand everything.
Just take the next step with Jesus.
Then the next one.
And the next one.

And one day, you'll look back and say—just like I did:

He lifted me.
He healed me.
He encouraged me.
He restored me.
He awakened me.

This is your moment.
Your season.
Your shift.
Your rising.

I am praying for you.
I am rooting for you.
And I believe in the woman God is calling you to be.

With love,
with understanding,
and with the same grace God showed me—

I bless your awakening.
You are H.E.R.
Healing.
Encouraged.
Restored.
Awakened by Jesus Christ.

If God awakened me, He can awaken you — right where you are.

-Evangelist Cher Randle

THE AWAKENING PRAYER

FINAL CHAPTER

Father God,

I come before You with a heart full of gratitude, surrender, and reverence for who You are and all You have done in my life. Thank You for awakening me, for lifting me, for healing me, for restoring me, and for revealing the woman You always saw within me. Thank You for Your patience, Your grace, Your mercy, and Your unfailing love.

Lord, as I pray over every woman reading this book, I ask You to awaken something new in her—something deep, something holy, something powerful. Stir her spirit in a way she has never felt before. Touch the hidden places she was afraid to expose. Speak to the wounds she has carried for years. Bring light into every dark corner and remind her that she is seen, known, and deeply loved by You.

God, breathe life into her identity.
Let her see herself the way You see her.
Let her walk boldly in the purpose You designed for her.
Let her release the pain, fear, and shame that have held her hostage.
Let her stand as the woman You ordained her to be long before life tried to quiet her voice.

Strengthen her heart, Lord.
Lift the heaviness that weighs her down.
Calm the storms that rage inside her.
Silence the lies the enemy whispers.
Break the chains of insecurity, comparison, and doubt.

Awaken joy where sorrow once lived.
Awaken peace where anxiety tried to take root.
Awaken confidence where fear once shut her down.
Awaken hope where disappointment tried to bury her dreams.

Reveal to her that she is not her past.
She is not her mistakes.
She is not her trauma.
She is not what people have called her.

She is Yours.

Father let her know that she is not awakening alone. You are with her in every step, every tear, every stretch, every surrender, and every transformation. You are guiding her into the woman she was created to be. Remind her that she does not have to be strong on her own, she only must be surrendered.

Lord, awaken her passion.
Awaken her purpose.
Awaken her confidence.
Awaken her voice.

Awaken her dreams.
Awaken her faith.
Awaken her strength.
Awaken her calling.

Cover her in Your presence.
Keep her anchored in Your Word.
Surround her with divine protection.
Align her with the right people, the right doors, and the right opportunities.
Let her walk in divine alignment, divine order, and divine purpose.

God, as You continue the work You have started in her, let her never forget that You are the One who lifts, heals, encourages, restores, and transforms. Let her awakening become a testimony that draws others to Your love.

I decree and declare that every woman reading this book will walk boldly in her healing, her encouragement, her restoration, and her awakening.
I decree and declare that chains are breaking, hearts are softening, minds are renewing, purpose is activating, and destiny is rising.

Lord, thank You for choosing me to write these words. Thank You for trusting me with this assignment. Thank You for awakening me so I can help awaken Your daughters.
And Father—
as long as I live,
my answer will always be:

"Jesus is the Answer.
That's it.
That's ALL."

In Jesus' name,
Amen.

This is not the end of your story; it is the beginning of your awakening.

-Evangelist Cher Randle

Dedication

THIS BOOK IS DEDICATED FIRST AND FOREVER TO JESUS CHRIST, MY SAVIOR, MY REDEEMER, MY HEALER, MY RESTORER, AND THE ONE WHO AWAKENED ME. EVERYTHING I AM, EVERYTHING I HAVE, AND EVERYTHING I WRITE IS BECAUSE OF HIM.

TO MY HUSBAND, MY CHILDREN, AND MY GRANDCHILDREN — THANK YOU FOR BEING MY REASON TO KEEP GOING, TO KEEP BELIEVING, AND TO KEEP TRUSTING GOD THROUGH EVERY SEASON. YOUR LOVE, PATIENCE, AND SUPPORT CARRIED ME THROUGH THE WOMAN I WAS AND EMBRACED THE WOMAN I WAS BECOMING.

TO MY MOTHER AND FATHER, THANK YOU FOR THE FOUNDATION YOU LAID, THE SACRIFICES YOU MADE, AND THE LOVE YOU POURED INTO ME. YOUR STRENGTH, FAITH, AND GUIDANCE SHAPED THE WOMAN I AM TODAY.

TO MY SIBLINGS, THANK YOU FOR YOUR LOVE, ENCOURAGEMENT, PRAYERS, AND SUPPORT ALONG THIS JOURNEY. WHETHER NEAR OR FAR, YOU HAVE BEEN PART OF MY STORY IN MORE WAYS THAN YOU KNOW.

TO EVERY LOVED ONE WHO BELIEVED IN ME, STOOD BY ME, PRAYED FOR ME, AND SUPPORTED ME — THANK YOU FOR LOVING ME THROUGH GROWTH, HEALING, AND AWAKENING.

TO EVERY WOMAN SEARCHING, HURTING, HEALING, OR RISING — THIS BOOK IS FOR YOU. MAY YOU FIND YOUR AWAKENING AND WALK BOLDLY IN WHO GOD CREATED YOU TO BE.

AND TO EVERY SISTER IN CHRIST WHO HAS EVER FELT UNSEEN, UNHEARD, OR UNWORTHY — MAY THIS BOOK REMIND YOU THAT GOD HAS ALWAYS HAD HIS EYES ON YOU.

Acknowldgments

I WANT TO THANK GOD ABOVE ALL — FOR HIS GRACE, HIS PATIENCE, HIS LOVE, AND HIS HAND ON MY LIFE. WITHOUT HIM, THERE WOULD BE NO BOOK, NO TESTIMONY, NO AWAKENING, AND NO PURPOSE.

TO MY INCREDIBLE FAMILY, THANK YOU FOR LOVING ME THROUGH SEASONS OF GROWTH AND TRANSFORMATION. YOU SAW ME WHEN I DIDN'T SEE MYSELF. YOUR PRAYERS, SUPPORT, AND ENCOURAGEMENT GAVE ME STRENGTH ON DAYS WHEN MY SPIRIT FELT WEAK.

TO EVERY WOMAN WHO WILL READ THESE PAGES — THANK YOU FOR TRUSTING ME WITH YOUR JOURNEY. THANK YOU FOR ALLOWING MY STORY TO SPEAK INTO YOURS. AND THANK YOU FOR BEING BRAVE ENOUGH TO HEAL, TO HOPE, TO RISE, AND TO AWAKEN.

TO EVERY MENTOR, LEADER, AND VOICE WHO POURED INTO ME — YOUR WISDOM IS WOVEN INTO MY AWAKENING. I HONOR YOU.

Made in the USA
Coppell, TX
20 January 2026

68683570R00031